MISS MYLES

A STACK

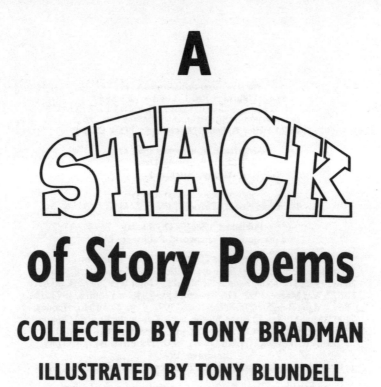

of Story Poems

COLLECTED BY TONY BRADMAN

ILLUSTRATED BY TONY BLUNDELL

DOUBLEDAY

LONDON . NEW YORK . TORONTO . SYDNEY . AUCKLAND

TRANSWORLD PUBLISHERS LTD
61–63 Uxbridge Road, London W5 5SA

TRANSWORLD PUBLISHERS (AUSTRALIA) PTY LTD
15-23 Helles Avenue, Moorebank, NSW 2170

TRANSWORLD PUBLISHERS (NZ) LTD
3 William Pickering Drive,
Albany, Auckland

DOUBLEDAY CANADA LTD
105 Bond Street, Toronto, Ontario M5B 1Y3

Published 1992 by Doubleday
a division of Transworld Publishers Ltd

A catalogue record for this book is available
from the British Library

ISBN 0 385 402155

Typeset by Falcon Graphic Art Ltd
Wallington, Surrey
Printed in Great Britain by
Mackays of Chatham Plc, Chatham, Kent

CONTENTS

BANDANNA BILL

Bandanna Bill, the Bandit Chief, was
   feeling really low;
He'd just run out of biscuits and right
   now it looked like snow.
He was cooped up in a cavern which
   was cold and caked with grime,
Eating nettle soup for supper for the
   forty-second time.

His trousers were in tatters and the sole
   hung off his shoe.
There was dirt beneath his fingernails
   (though that was nothing new).
By now he should be well-to-do, like
   every other bandit,
So why then was he stony-broke? He
   couldn't understand it.

(The aim should be, in banditry, to end
  up *stinking rich*,
Not slinking round on mountaintops or
  skulking in a ditch.
Ill-gotten gains are vital. They will get
  you out of caverns –
Into continental holidays and five-course
  meals in taverns.)

His men, of course, were grumbling. They
  were a surly group.
They sat around and moaned about the
  weather and the soup
And the rising cost of living and the
  squalor and the chill,
But most of all they moaned about their
  boss, Bandanna Bill.

There was Desperado Davey, there was
  Mongo, there was Nobby,
There was Christopher the Creepy who
  kept spiders for a hobby.
There was Spud the Masked Potato, there
  was Raging Reg O'Rourke,
There was Hank the Hand and Bert the
  Boot and crazy Mack the Fork.

Yes, times were hard for bandits. There
    just wasn't much to steal.
A shepherd's pickle sandwich hardly makes
    a decent meal.
No point in robbing peasants – each was
    poorer than the last,
And the travellers that came their way
    had learned to leg it – *fast!*

No, what Bill really needed was a bold,
     dramatic plan.
A cunning plan that worked a treat, the
     way a good plan can.
Or better still, a stroke of luck. A travelling
     millionaire
Or perhaps a helpless princess. Either one.
     He didn't care.

Just then the lookout scuttled in. His
     name was Crosseyed Ted.
'Two coaches fast approachin' up the
     mountain path!' he said.
(Poor Ted had trouble with his sight and
     always saw in two's.
This caused a lot of merriment but tended
     to confuse.)

'Go count the coaches, Spud!' barked Bill.
     'Boys, this could be our chance!
It's goodbye cave on mountaintop and
     hello South of France!
Just follow me, lads. I'm the boss. I'll
     show you how it's done.'
Spud raced back with the heady news.
     A coach approached! (Just one.)

4

The bandits grabbed their weapons then
  and hurried from the cave.
Bandanna Bill, then Mongo, Spud and
  Desperado Dave.
And next came Chris the Creepy with
  his usual sort of leer,
Close followed by the others. (Mack the
  Fork brought up the rear.)

They hid about behind the rocks the way
  that bandits do
And very soon an ancient coach came
  rattling into view.
The coachman was a grim old man who
  smoked a smelly pipe;
He never washed and never spoke (an
  anti-social type).

5

The horse had found the slope a strain
   (it was more used to town).
It saw the bandits up ahead and gratefully
   slowed down.
Just then an icy voice rang out. 'What's
   going on?' it said.
And from the coach's window poked an
   irate female head.

'Who are these grim and grubby men
   who clearly need a wash?'
'We're bandits,' said Bandanna Bill, 'and
   what we want is dosh.'
'How dare you!' said the steely voice.
   'Don't you know who I am?
I'm Pamela de Vinderburg. They call me
   Lady Pam.'

The door crashed back and down she
   stepped. Her eyes were blue and blazing.
Bandanna Bill went hot and cold like
   faulty double glazing.
She glared directly at him with a most
   indignant air.
His legs went weak and wobbly – he
   wished he had a chair.

6

Now Lady Pam was stern and small and
    didn't give an inch.
She'd fight a mountain lion – or a couple,
    at a pinch.
She had a rolled umbrella with a special
    sharpened tip,
And she held on to her handbag with
    a most determined grip.

'Now, what is all this nonsense? Hurry
   up, because I'm late.
Take your hands out of your pockets,
   man! And try to stand up straight.
Turn out your toes, don't pick your nose
   and think before you speak.
I want an explanation and I haven't got
   all week.'

(When Lady Pam was pressed for time,
   she didn't suffer fools.
She did a lot for orphans and she sat
   on boards in schools.
She was always very busy with collections
   and appeals.
She took pensioners on outings and
   delivered meals on wheels.)

'I told you,' said Bandanna Bill. He
   sounded ill at ease.
'I said we wants yer money. Er – your
   bag, milady? Please?'
But he said it very sheepishly. His voice
   was low and muffled.
He hung his head and turned bright red.
   He coughed a bit and shuffled.

'D'you realize,' snapped Lady Pam, 'that
    while you talk of gold,
Right at this moment in the coach, *ten
    meals* are getting cold?
That while you stand there talking with
    your nasty bandit mates,
Ten hungry old-age pensioners are fainting
    at their plates?

That schools are busy closing due to
    limited resources?
And so are donkey sanctuaries and homes
    for aged horses?
I'm really very busy, and I just don't
    have the time
To stand around and listen to you brutes
    who stoop to crime.

It's time you smartened up a bit and
    tidied up your cave.
It's time you bought a toothbrush and
    it's time you had a shave.
You ought to be ashamed, you did! Great
    hulking brutes like you,
Depriving poor old people of their chicken
    vindaloo.

9

And if you think,' she finished, 'that I'll
    give you lazy lot
One penny of this money, I assure you,
    I will not.
This money is intended to buy orphans
    central heating.
And now, if you'll excuse me, I must
    rush. I have a meeting.'

The bandits didn't say a word. Big Mongo
    hung his head
And Nobby bit his fingernails, and so
    did Crosseyed Ted.
And Christopher the Creepy tried to slink
    behind a tree
In the vain hope that her ladyship just
    maybe wouldn't see.

'One moment,' said Bandanna Bill. His
    eyes were wet with tears.
'I'd like to help them orphans, see. Poor
    lonely little dears.
I'd like to buy 'em sugar plums and lots
    o' lovely toys.
Us bandits ain't so bad at heart. Turn
    out your pockets, boys.'

And so, while Lady Pamela got her
    collecting tin,
The bandits searched about themselves for
    something to put in.
Crosseyed Ted found twopence, which
    he later claimed was four,
Big Mongo found a marble and a stamp
    from Singapore.

There were buttons, pencils, peppermints
and lumps of chewing gum,
And Spud the Masked Potato had a photo
of his mum
And Nobby found a toffee in a grubby
paper bag.
Quite an interesting collection, but you
couldn't call it swag.

There were seven dirty handkerchiefs and
lots of other stuff
Such as chicken bones and lucky stones
and loads and loads of fluff.
They stood around and looked at it. There
wasn't much to say.
It was pitifully obvious that Crime Just
Does Not Pay.

'I'm sorry, Lady Pam,' said Bill. He was
    apologetic.
'That's all we got, that little heap. I know
    it looks pathetic.
We'd like to give donations to the causes
    you support
But business ain't too good, you see. This
    week, we're kind of short.'

'In that case,' said her ladyship, 'I've
    something to suggest.
Give up this life of banditry! That really
    would be best.
Get jobs! Go straight! It's not too late!
    Great strapping men like you!
To start with, you can work for me.
    I'll find you things to do.'

And that is how Bandanna Bill and Raging
    Reg O'Rourke
And Hank the Hand and Ben the Boot
    and crazy Mack the Fork
And all the other ruffians gave up their
    old careers
To work for Lady Pamela as willing
    volunteers.

She taught them how to be polite and
  have determined chins
And how to leap on passers-by with huge
  collecting tins.
She threw away their daggers and their
  cudgels and their axes
And she dressed them all in blazers and
  she made them pay their taxes.

Bandanna Bill, when washed and brushed
  and buttoned in a suit,
Looked altogether different and somehow
  sort of cute.
He took up the recorder and he learned
  to be a waiter.
He married Lady Pam, of course – but
  that was much, much later.

Kaye Umansky

TOM'S GUINEA PIG

'First day of Spring tomorrow,'
Miss Bell had said.
Sky's now like a feather bed,
Grubby, hanging too low,
Bursting with snow.
Furred with frost,
The spiders' webs show.
Flowers and green are all in hiding,
No ice though . . . so no sliding.
Except for our anoraks all's grey.
No football, not much play
Before school.
We're all sniffing,
Aching thumbs ready to burst
With cold
On this first day of Spring.

15

At last we're in.
Pipes clanking, radiators very hot,
Lights dispel the grey.
Spring? Oh no it's not.
Outside and in – a winter's day.
But we sang 'Morning has broken'
As if we'd done the breaking
And Miss Bell, as a token
Of welcome to Spring,
Banged the piano
Joyfully.
Winter might be leaving a little late, she
    said,
But Spring would come soon,
Perhaps an anticyclone that very afternoon.
So the second verse soared into the warm air
As if we believed her.
(We have to take care
Of Miss Bell now. She's getting on.)

Suddenly Tom made his mouth a square,
A huge, red, dark space
In his face,
And howled as babies can.
Tears dripped, collected and ran
Down to his collar.

16

The singing sagged, then stopped
And we all stared at Tom.
His face stretched, his jaw dropped
And he cried out loud again.
Hearing him
Made us flinch.
Jane began to snivel.
(She catches crying as the rest of us catch
   colds.)
'Cor!' Now there's two of 'em!' Sid said.
'I'm gorn home. Too damp in here.
Anybody comin'?'
And most of us giggled.
I glared but Sid pretended not to see.
Sometimes I think he likes Lynne
More than me.

Behind the piano,
Still joyful and out of sight,
Miss Bell banged on with all her might
And when again Tom bawled
She called,
'Come along all of you . . . sing!
Believe it's Spring.
Stand proud.'
So I said pretty loud,
'Miss Bell!'
And she heard.
Without a word
She gave Jane a tissue
And put an arm round Tom.
Her eyes slid
Over the rest of us,
Settled on Sid.
'Anyone know what's the matter?'
None of us could guess,
Not even Tess
Whose mother knows everything about
    everybody.
'How should I know?' she blustered.
She looked so flustered
I thought she'd howl.
'I reckon he's jest upset,' Sid drawled,

And even Miss Bell smiled.
Then Tom yelped and sobbed
And kept on.
I couldn't stop looking at his mouth,
Squarc and red.
'Why don't you shut up?' Sid said.
And suddenly Tom, that great mouth gone,
His crying done,
Muttered, 'I'm OK.'
Made a pillow of his arms,
Tucked his wet face away
And was still and quiet.

We all wrote then,
Stories and reports to use
With local news
In our magazine.
The editor's Miss Bell.

19

Now and then while she read
She walked near Tom, touched his head,
And once he spoke
But none of us heard.
George reckoned Tom had bellyache.
Jane said his family were dead.
'She's crackers,' Derek said
And we laughed a bit,
But nobody felt cheerful, Spring or not.
We like Tom nearly always.
Though he's big he doesn't bully.
He plays fair and knows all about trees. . .
More than Miss Bell
(She agrees).
He could ask his mum
(She's our dinner lady)
For extra chips
But he never does.
(He wouldn't get them
Because she's fair.)
'I think it's something serious,'
Karen whispered very low.
'What d'you mean?' I said.
She shows off. I knew she didn't know.
Just some words she'd heard.
Absurd!

20

Miss Bell collected our copy
And very softly, looking at us, said,
'Patch, Tom's guinea pig, is dead.'
But Tom heard every word
And, though I could see
He tried not to cry aloud,
He did
And we all jumped,
Even Sid.
Tom pumped
Great rivulets of tears
Down his poor face.
Then down went his head again
And he was still.
'Fancy howling over a guinea pig!
Must be nuts,' Sid said.
'Certainly making a fuss,' added Lynne.
I felt my face go red.
'S'pose it was Finn?'
I said. Finn's Sid's dog.
He glared at me.
'Shut up. Dogs are different.
And, by the way, his name is Finnegan.'
Derek slid a black wine gum under Tom's
    elbow
But Tom didn't stir, didn't know.

21

It was still untouched at break.
It seemed a waste. . .
I love blackcurrant taste.

Break over, it was science . . . in groups.
Lovely things we had.
Copper sulphate, soda, beakers, pipettes
    and test tubes.
Tom's in our group and I was sad,
Glad
I hadn't taken that wine gum
Because he sat alone.
Everyone loves science, even Joan,
But Tom sat still as a stone.
Then suddenly he raised his head. . .
No awful noises though.
His face was soaking wet and red
And his eyes were slits,
The brown bits
Peering through fat lids.
He had hiccups too
And could barely speak.
With one hand full of growing crystals,
Miss Bell put the other
On his shoulder.
'We're so sorry, Tom, that Patch is dead,'
She said.

'I killed him.'
Tom's voice was hoarse.
'Forgot to fasten the latch
On the hutch
And cover the roof.
There was a frost . . . not much . . .
But Patch was small.
He was still and stiff this morning.'
We were all a bit miserable but only Jane
    cried
Until I thumped her.
'Pack up quietly,' Miss Bell said,
Gave me the crystals
And sat and talked to Tom.

It was very quiet and we all heard the
    door open.
We stared.
Our school's small and we notice visitors.
Tom's mum stood in the doorway.
Too early for dinner.
Besides, she wore ordinary clothes,
Looked thinner
Without her white overall.
She held the corner of an apron
Rolled round something small

In her left hand, cuddling it close against
    her.
You could almost touch the quiet in the
    room.
'Tom,' she said, 'come and see.'
He rose,
Rubbed his sleeve across his nose
And stumbled out to her.
Tom's mum let down the corner of her
    apron
And we belted out to see. . .
And there was Patch,
Twitching his nose, peering round, very
    frisky.
'I reckon he's looking for more of my
    whisky,'
Tom's mum said . . . and laughed.
We all laughed then and couldn't stop,
Even Miss Bell.
'Well,' she said. 'Well!'
Even Sid grinned
And I've never seen anything as joyful
    as Tom's face.
It was red and puffy and streaked with grey
But it was birthday and breaking up and
    Christmas Day

All at once,
Though he still had hiccups.
Tom's mum wrapped the apron round
   Patch,
Gave him to Tom.
'Keep him warm,' she said.
'Took me all morning to get him right.'
Her eyes were very bright.
'Thanks, Mum,' Tom said
And kissed her.
I quelled Jane with a look.

Then Tom gave Patch to Sid to hold
While he washed his face.
Came back pink and fierce and bold
As though he'd never howled in his life.

'Why don't you get a dog?' Sid said.
'Yeah, why not?' echoed Lynne.
'Prefer bitches,' Tom said. 'Ours'll have
    pups soon.'
And for once Sid was speechless.
And Lynne . . . well, I smiled at her.

While Tom's mum fetched her overall
We all held Patch
So that we could stroke
That little creature
Who'd been nearly dead.
'Used an eye-dropper, I did,'
Tom's mum told us, serving shepherd's pie,
And Jane, who never says anything
    sensible,
Gave a chirpy little cry.
'We use them in science.
They suck up and measure drops,'
She announced.
And even George stopped eating.
Then we laughed . . . a long laugh.
And it was easy to believe it was the
    first day of Spring.

Gwen Dunn

26

THE NATTY KNIGHT
SIR NIGEL

Sir Nigel was a natty knight
Who liked to keep his armour bright.
He polished up his suit of metal
Till shiny as a copper kettle.
(It took a lot of elbow grease
To polish every single piece.)

When other knights went off to wars,
Sir Nigel could be found indoors;
While other knights their foes demolished,
Sir Nigel just stayed home and polished;
And every nut and bolt and screw
All came up looking good as new.

Now one day, when some other knights
Returned from gruesome battle sites,
They thought they might be welcomed
   home,
But Nigel just cried, 'Mind my chrome!
It's bright and shiny, not like yours
That's scuffed and scratched through
   fighting wars!'

Of course, his fellow knights were vexed
And wondered what he might say next.
Sir Nigel, having thought a bit,
Then added, 'While I think of it,
I hope no-one expects to borrow
My metal-cleaning stuff tomorrow!'
Then just to show he was well bred,
He said, 'Good-night' and went to bed.

Sir John, Sir Jasper and Sir Paul
Were dumbstruck by Sir Nigel's gall.
Sir Hector and Sir Ethelred
Could scarce believe the things he'd said.
Sir Desmond and Sir Dominic
Were left there, feeling pretty sick.

Now when they'd gathered up their wits,
Said John: 'We mustn't call it quits!'
They sat and wondered what to do
To bring him down a peg or two.
They pondered hard and by next day
Between them, they'd worked out a way.

They made a great big dragon skin
From bits of wood and glass and tin.
They made it tall enough and wide
For all of them to fit inside.
Great puffs of purple smoke came out
The nostrils each side of its snout.
Its mouth was fearsome, breathing flame,
Its teeth were sharp, its claws the same.
Its fourteen legs had lots of scales,
Its bottom was as hard as nails.
In short, it was a ghastly sight,
Enough to give grown men a fright,
Not least of all Sir Nigel, who
Was scared of spiders in the loo.

The seven knights thus underneath
The dragon costume, with its teeth
And claws and scales and fiery breath,
Thought they'd scare Nigel half to death,
And even if he wasn't hurt,
At least he'd grovel in the dirt
And spoil his spotless suit of steel.
And what a fool he's sure to feel
When he finds out it's all a hoax
And just one of their little jokes!

They waited for Sir Nigel, knowing
That soon to market he'd be going
To buy a tin of Duraglit,
As he was getting short of it.
With bated breath at half-past three
They hid behind a chestnut tree,
And tittered to themselves and thought:
Oh, what a lesson he'll be taught!

Quite soon Sir Nigel came in sight,
Proud in his suit of armour bright.
Just as he passed the chestnut tree
The 'dragon' jumped out suddenly.
Like something from a nasty dream
It looked, and boy, did Nigel scream!

But then one knight, Sir Ethelred,
Inside the dragon's hollow head,
Whose job it was to work the smoke,
Inhaled some and began to choke,
And then with one almighty cough
He blew the costume's head clean off!

Sir Nigel, who was much surprised
To see this face he recognized,
Then saw it all was but a game.
The mighty monster now seemed tame:
A dragon who had lost its head
And got a human one instead!
Sir Nigel laughed and cried, 'Baloney!
This monster's nothing but a phoney!'

The seven knights were rather miffed
Their clever plan had gone adrift,
And went home without much to say
As Nigel went upon his way.

This could have been the way it ends,
But no, the road was full of bends.
The outcome couldn't be forlorner:
Behind a rock, around the corner,
A real–life dragon (looking thinner
Than it ought through lack of dinner)
Was waiting for some poor dimwit
To come by, to be ate by it.

Sir Nigel came, he saw, he giggled.
Sir Nigel got the dragon niggled.
He thought, This dragon's also fake,
Which was, of course, a grave mistake.
He laughed aloud until he buckled.
'I'll not be fooled again!' he chuckled.

The dragon couldn't see the joke,
And breathing fire and belching smoke,
It opened up its jaws and ate
Sir Nigel and his armour plate.

Colin West

THE GREEN GIRL

A boy named Dean MacKendrick
and his young sister Fran,
were to spend a winter weekend
with Grandad Throakes and Nan.
Mum and Dad would take them there
in the family's Escort van.

'I won't go without a friend,'
moaned Dean. He looked quite cross.
Fran frowned and said, 'Me neither.'
Their mum was at a loss.
She shrugged: 'OK, but don't forget
that Grandad Throakes is boss!'

Fran ran to ask Jamila,
and Dean asked 'Rapper' Rule.
What had seemed a dull weekend
now suddenly looked cool.
All gathered at MacKendrick's house
on Friday, after school.

The van left Spitfire Crescent
on Lancaster Estate
and reached the Yorkshire village
as it was getting late.
Nan welcomed them with mugs of tea.
A fire flared in the grate.

Grandad Throakes puffed on his pipe.
His beard was white as snow.
Dad drank his tea, then clinked his keys,
and Mum said, 'Time to go.'
Nan saw them to the front gate
and called, 'Enjoy the show!'

The Throakes' stone house was massive.
It stood three storeys tall.
A clock ticked on the landing.
Antlered hatstand in the hall.
The attic was the boys' room;
grey cobwebs on the wall.

The girls pushed back their bedroom door.
It opened with a squeak.
'It's spooky,' said Jamila,
'and don't the floorboards creak!'
They gazed out through the window,
viewed the village . . . dark and bleak.

Hours later – way past midnight –
a sudden cry woke Dean.
He lay still in his sleeping bag.
What had he heard? A scream?
Beside him . . . Rapper snoring.
Was it him? Or just a dream?

At breakfast Dean told everyone
about the scary sound.
While Nan served eggs and bacon,
he said – and here he frowned –
'The cry came from far away,
like somewhere . . . underground.'

The girls and Rapper half froze
but Grandad Throakes, good host,
smiled gently and spread butter
on a doorstep slice of toast.
'I think,' he softly said to Dean,
'you 'eard our cellar ghost.'

Dust settled on the table.
Feet wriggled in their socks.
Rapper gulping bacon, said,
'It could have been a fox.'
Grandad slowly shook his head,
from the sideboard took a box

and opened it, withdrew a key.
'This fits the cellar door,'
he said. 'Why don't you 'ave a look,
go down there and explore?
Yon ghost's supposed to walk,' he
    grinned,
'below this kitchen floor.'

'It's said,' continued Grandad,
'one night o' howlin' gale,
a child were caught i' Cryer's Wood
and wolf-like was 'er wail.
Bare she was, and wild, and wan.'
'What's wan mean?' Fran asked.
                              'Pale.'

Grandad held his gnarled hands wide
and talked on, soft and low.
'Story goes, they brought 'er 'ere,
t' cellar, down below.
Course,' he coughed, 'it all took place
a century ago.'

'Doctor were called to see 'er,
declared 'er 'alf-insane.
She wouldn't speak, just whimpered,
like an animal i' pain.
Twas said she lived wi' creatures
i' wood . . . i' snow and rain.'

The children's questions tumbled
across the breakfast spread.
'Who was she?' and 'How old?'
'I don't know,' Grandad said.
'But there are those who've 'eard 'er cry.
Not me. Yon child's long dead.'

Nan said, 'Oh, stop your nonsense.
You'll make Fran fret and cry.
Off with you . . . to the village shop!'
Poor Grandad heaved a sigh.
Outside, fine rain was falling
and dark clouds filled the sky.

Fran, Jamila, Rapper, Dean
discussed what they should do.
Exploration of the cellar,
all agreed, was overdue.
'Let's go see,' said Dean, 'and prove
the legend false . . . or true.'

The wall clock on the landing
dull-struck the hour of ten
as Dean turned the rusty key.
He shoved the door . . . and then
a musty smell came wafting up:
old clothes . . . a lion's den!

Dean had borrowed Grandad's torch,
for the cellar had no light.
Its thin beam probed the darkness
like a laser in the night.
The children saw worn stone steps,
a steep, descending flight.

One by one they ventured down
into that inky gloom,
and one by one reached the floor
of a tiny, rough-walled room.
Dean whispered, 'Must be what it's like
to be buried in a tomb.'

The torch threw light on tea chests,
cobwebbed bottles – beer and wine.
The children crept, crept forward
like blind men down a mine,
and Fran felt a shivery chill
run up and down her spine.

Six rooms made up the cellar,
each walled with Yorkshire stone.
The musty air was damp and cold.
It struck right to the bone.
Rapper Rule banged his head
and gave an anguished groan.

Jamila heard a squeaking.
She whimpered, 'What was that?'
Dean grinned, and told the girls,
'Oh, probably a bat.'
Fran saw horrors in her mind
. . . dread spider, mouse and rat!

Fearful, they searched the cellar,
each room a darkened hole.
They found a sink, a dripping tap,
pile of forgotten coal.
'Down here,' said Rapper ruefully,
'I feel just like a mole.'

Dean chuckled at him, then said,
'There's no ghost here. Let's go.'
He walked towards the stone steps
but tripped and hurt his toe.
He dropped the torch. The light went out.
Dean's voice cried, 'No! Oh, no!'

The four stood in the darkness
and a silence filled the air.
Fran grabbed Jamila's arm.
'There's a spider in my hair!'
The four felt as if . . . as if . . .
someone else was there.

Dean suddenly moved forward
towards the stone steps' flight
but found himself stopped in his tracks
by a dim, diffusing light
which spread throughout the cellar.
The four stood filled with fright.

Four hearts thumped, eyes strained to see,
amazed mouths opened wide.
The children saw a moving shape
. . . it seemed to float . . . to glide.
Panic-stricken, Fran looked round
for a place where she could hide.

The lambent light took on a form,
a child with green-tinged skin,
and tousled hair, a wild-eyed look,
and legs and arms . . . stick-thin.
Dean felt himself grow giddy,
his brain was in a spin.

The green-skinned girl now uttered
a stark wail of despair
and once again Dean heard the sound
that caused him last night's scare.
And then, before his staring eyes,
she vanished in thin air.

Up the steps the children shot
like bullets from a gun
and raced into the kitchen
where Nan asked, "ad good fun?
Look, Grandad's bought for each of you
a fresh-baked, cream-filled bun.'

Dean, Jamila, Rapper, Fran
in the kitchen sat aghast,
hearing in their heads that cry
– wolf-wail from decades past –
and even now, cream buns in hand,
their hearts were beating fast.

Grandad Throakes, pipe belching smoke,
looked at the children, smiled.
'Well,' he said, 'did you see 'er then?'
He chortled. 'Was she wild?
It's a right rum story, that 'un,
about yon poor young child.'

Dean glanced up at the others,
but no-one said a word.
He knew they'd keep the secret
of what they'd seen and heard.
'Sorry Grandad. Lost your torch.'
The truth was best left blurred.

The hours ticked by that Saturday,
and the children sat, sat still.
Nan asked them if they felt all right,
and were they feeling ill?
'Yon cellar,' she scolded Grandad,
''as given them a chill!'

That night, in his sleeping bag,
Dean listened for the cry,
but in the attic silence reigned
while a full moon sailed the sky.
For Sunday breakfast Nan served up
boiled eggs and sausage pie.

Rapper, Fran, Jamila, Dean
decided not to tell
about the ghostly, green-skinned girl
and the cellar where Dean fell.
They agreed to keep the secret
of the wild girl in her cell.

That evening Mum and Dad returned.
Mum asked, 'How's things? OK?'
The children nodded. Nan said,
'I was pleased to 'ave them stay.
So well behaved and 'elpful,
and so quiet yesterday.'

Dad said they should be shifting
as it was getting late.
The four piled in the Escort.
The Throakes waved from the gate.
The van sped off for Spitfire Cres.
on Lancaster Estate.

The weekend trip was over.
The four trudged off to bed,
where visions of the green girl
lived on in each child's head.
Exhausted, Dean slept deeply,
flat out like someone dead.

Fran, Jamila, Rapper, Dean
hoped one day they'd return
to Nan's house in the village
where with good luck they'd learn
more about the cellar ghost.
Alas, their wish was spurned

for Nan and Grandad sold up,
moved to a bungalow,
their old house bought by people
the family didn't know.
The green girl's ghost lay shrouded
like a garden under snow.

★

But. . .

exactly one year later,
as Dean lay fast asleep,
a sudden cry woke the boy.
It made his young flesh creep.
He heard the green girl . . . in his house!
He heard her wail and weep.

Next day he told the others.
Fran said, 'You *saw* her, here?'
'Didn't *see* the ghost,' said Dean,
'but I *heard* her, loud and clear.
Since that meeting in the cellar
it's – to the day – one year!'

Would the ghost return each year
to haunt them, friend by friend?
And if the green girl did come back
what did her cry portend?
As Dean remarked, 'Perhaps this is
a story without end. . .'

Wes Magee

THE GRATEFUL LION
A Moral Tale

A long time ago, on the outskirts of Rome,
There once lived a man and his wife.
He rounded up strays, which he'd then
   take back home,
To give them a new start in life.

His wife threw her arms up and loudly
   complained
On seeing his first little mouse.
She just didn't care that its ankle was
   sprained.
'I'm not having that in the house!

It's nasty and noisy and vicious,' she cried;
'It's eyeing the larder with greed.
For heaven's sake stamp on it, throw it
   outside!
It'll cost us a fortune to feed.'

Although he was timid, the man stood
   his ground,
And got out the ointment and lint;
And lifting the foot up, he bandaged it
   round
And straightened it out with a splint.

'You just wait and see, dear,' he said
   when he'd done,
'In less than a week he'll be fine;
He won't want much more than the odd
   currant bun.
I'm sure he's quite welcome to mine.'

Well, that was the first but it wasn't the last:
The next stage was bats in the loo.
At each new arrival his wife was aghast;
'This house is becoming a zoo!

The sitting-room's crowded with wild
   parakeets,
White rabbits are filling the sink;
We've toads in the towels and snakes in
   the sheets –
And the carpets are starting to stink!'

Although he kept silent, he had to agree.
Embarrassed, he nibbled his cake.
He'd only half house-trained that last
   chimpanzee,
And the warthog had been a mistake.

She lifted him up by his Roman lapels;
Her sides were beginning to heave.
'I'm sick of the noise and the fleas and
   the smells,'
She bawled. 'Turf them out – or I leave!'

The offer was tempting; alas, he lacked
    nerve.
His voice came out strangled and tight:
'I'll just give them supper – the least they
    deserve –
And send them off into the night.'

He watched them depart and he silently
    grieved;
His heart was like lead with regrets.
His wife smiled in triumph for, so she
    believed,
She'd now seen the last of his pets.

*

One night, some months later, a howl
    and a scratch
Set both of them trembling with fear.
'There's something outside and it's lifting
    the latch,'
She gasped; 'and it's coming in here!'

The door was flung open, a lion limped
  inside
And showed them his paw, with a lick.
'You must lend a hand, dear; it's too
  late to hide;
Please bring me the first-aid box, quick!

The poor creature's hurt,' said the man
  to his wife.
He then told the lion, 'It's all right.
I'll ease out that thorn with the point
  of my knife.'
His wife said, 'He can't stay the night.'

The job was soon over. No longer in pain
The lion gave a smile of content.
He purred as he rubbed the man's legs
  with his mane;
But he scowled at the wife as he went.

Time passed, as it has to; they never
   complained,
Despite all the jobs to be done.
The man did his woodwork whenever
   it rained
And tended his fields in the sun.

And though he fed carrots to all the
   young hares
And smuggled out milk for the cat,
And rescued old blankets to warm up
   the bears,
His wife never knew about that.

One evening he got home to find that
   his wife
Was making herself a new dress.
'I've just had,' she said, 'the surprise of
   my life;
And what it is, you'll never guess.

They've sent us two tickets, and don't
   ask me why,
To visit the circus, for free,
On Saturday next. I'm so touched I could
   cry.
Now shut up; get on with your tea.'

The husband looked doubtful, he couldn't
  enthuse;
He wanted to say, 'It's not right.
I don't hold with circuses, pet-shops and
  zoos;'
But just held his tongue and sat tight.

★

The day of the outing they packed up some
  food
And started their journey to Rome.
The man was reluctant, just not in the
  mood:
He wished that he could have stayed home.

His wife led the way and declared, out
  of breath,
'Don't dawdle; stop dragging your feet!
You look like a man who's been sentenced
  to death –
Trust you to go spoiling our treat.'

Though thousands of people had come
  to the show,
A helpful young guard at the gate
Escorted them down to the very first row,
And thanked them for not being late.

The wife settled down with her packet
  of nuts.
'I do love the circus; it's grand
To see all those prisoners stabbed in the guts
And bleeding to death on the sand;

Or savaged by lions, or dragged through
  the dust
By stallions.' She dabbed at her eye.
'Yes, call me a tender old fool if you must;
I really enjoy a good cry.'

The wife beamed with pleasure; the
  husband was glum
(In fact, he was feeling quite ill).
'I do wish,' he said, 'you'd not forced
  me to come:
I fear that we're first on the bill.'

The guard gave the couple some helpful
  advice:
'Just keep on the move, that's the trick.
Run right round the back of the stalls
  once or twice;
They boo if it's over too quick.

And tremble and holler, and that sort
  of thing.'
The wife looked decidedly wan.
The guard pushed the two of them into
  the ring
And cheerfully whispered, 'You're on!'

A cage clattered open, a lion appeared
And let out an almighty roar.
The crowd waved their rattles and whistled
  and cheered.
The wife just collapsed on the floor.

The lion now was clearly preparing to
    spring
(At this point the audience went wild),
When suddenly – here's a remarkable
    thing –
It waggled its paw, and then smiled.

The man wiped his forehead and patted
    the beast
(They still talk about this in Rome),
And, leaving the lion to get on with its
    feast,
His bad-tempered wife, he went home.

★

I leave it to you to imagine the rest:
The lion and the man often met.
The tale has a moral, you probably guessed;
But just what it is, I forget.

John Yeoman

THE BOY AND THE BOGGART

Part 1

Once a young boggart lived on a farm.
Long, long ago, farms were full of such
  folk.
Some were helpful, others did harm:
hobgoblins, for instance, were really no
  joke;
brounies would help if you treated them
  right;
but boggarts! Well, boggarts might not
  – or they might.

But not our hairy boggart lad!
He had always too much fun
being *bad*.

59

He'd scatter the hens
to see them run,
pluck the cock's tail feathers
one by one,
drive nearly mad
the bull on his chain
– and then he'd do it all again.

He'd play such tricks as he was able
after supper in the stable:
tie the horses' tails in knots,
tangle all their heavy manes,
spill the oats and stale the water,
rust the bits and hide the reins.

A boggart's life is a merry one!
He does what he will and he cares for none.

He liked to play jokes on the farmer's wife.
'That boggart,' she cried, 'is the bane
     of my life!
He spoils my cheeses and turns the milk
     sour,
stops the butter from coming for hour
     after hour!'

The boggart thought it was very funny
to snatch their toys from the children's clasp
or, whisking the food from their startled
   grasp,
to drop in the mud their bread and honey.
He sniggered when they complained and
   cried.
Their mother, though, was fit to be tied.

She went to her man: ''Twas enough and
   too much
when the boggart just bothered the poor
   beasts and such.
Now 'tis the bairns! But I'll not have
   them frit.
There's nought for it, husband, but we
   must all flit.'

At sunset, in secret, and breathless with
   worry,
they loaded the carts in a flurry and scurry
with the beds, pots and pans, the chairs
   and the table,
all their clothes and some food and the
   grandfather clock,

the churns from the dairy, the gear from
   the stable,
the cat (in a sack) and four hens and the cock
and that evening's milk in the wife's
   biggest crock.

They harnessed the horses with stealthiest
   speed,
hushing each other, 'Take care!' and 'Pay
   heed!'
Then: 'Farewell to the house and the fields
   and the rest;
and farewell above all to the boggart,
   that pest!'

They creaked down the lane and had
   reached the last turn
where they splashed through the stream
   and brushed through the fern,
when a neighbour, out late, called, 'I hear
   you are quitting!'
And, lifting the lid of the big butter churn,
the boggart peered out to say, 'Oh aye,
   we're flitting!'

Back they all went, the farmer, his wife,
their children and cat to their hob-ridden
   life.

Oh, that boggart's life was a merry one!
He did as he chose and he cared for none.

Part 2

For many long years the boggart lived
   there,
playing his tricks to the mortals' despair.
The children grew up; the farmer grew old;
their boggart slowly grew less bold.
Then the old farmer died and his son Fred
took over the farm (and the boggart)
   instead.

The boggart grew lazy and let them alone.
For years he'd keep still till they thought
   he had gone –
Then! Here he'd be, teasing the dog with
   a bone;
there he'd be, chasing the hens here and
   yon.
'Drat that old boggart!' the farmer would
   sigh.
'Boggarts seemingly never die.'

And time went by and time went by.

Farmers came and farmers went;
some could hardly pay the rent.
Others grew rich in spite of his tricks
with fine fat beasts and full fat ricks;
while the boggart snoozed and the days
   slipped by,
the weeks and the months and the years
   whipped by.

For the boggart's life was a carefree one;
He did as he would and he heeded none.

Then:
The village downalong started to grow.
The boggart didn't care to know.
But then the village became a town
and gobbled the fields
turning green to brown.
And the trees in the copse were all cut
    down.

The town came closer, grabbing and
    swelling,
every meadow cut up for dwelling.
The town got louder and nearer still.
It swallowed the stream
and the watermill.
Then the boggart woke up and could
    see no hill.

Nothing but houses, row on row,
where the sweet grass used to grow;
smoke and grime and factory whistles;
the boggart even missed the thistles.

His people were gone, to the boggart's
    dismay,
and all their clutter was swept away.
The house was for sale! No longer a farm,
just a house and a garden, outhouses,
    a barn,
without any mod cons, mains water or
    drains!
Who'd want the mere shell of a house
    for his pains?

So the farmhouse stood bare;
    on the cold hearth no fire.
Out in the yard
    no cows in the byre,
no hens in the henhouse,
    no dog to give cry,
no hay in the hayloft,
    no pigs in the sty,
no horse in the stable,
    no cock's tail to pluck;
even the midden
    was empty of muck.

Oh, the boggart's life was a dreary one,
miserably boring, without any fun.

And, with no-one there to believe in him,
the boggart was growing weak and dim;
he was drying up like an autumn leaf,
fading away for lack of belief.

'I'll flit,' said the boggart,
    'I'll go somewhere new.
I'll leave this dull hole.
    What else can I do?'

The old boggart staggered out into the rain.
Down by the gate, driven deep in the
    mould,
stood the board with 'For Sale' on – but
    now it said SOLD!
People were coming to live here again!
The boggart gave a great sigh of relief.
He would stay and grow strong on the
    mortals' belief.

Part 3

First there came huge machines to dig,
clawing the earth for the sewers and drains;
machines to mix concrete, noisy and big,
machines to move pipes for the water
    mains.

The boggart was deafened, bewildered and
    scared;
motors revved up, men shouted, horns
    blared.
Wherever he turned there was uproar and
    strife.
The boggart began to fear for his life!

In desperation the boggart crept
into the house; was nearly swept
up by the roaring Hoover, fled
and hid himself beneath a bed,
trembling, battered with the din.
Then suddenly he heard a thin
wail that he knew. A baby? Here?
He crawled out, ready to disappear.

When no-one answered the baby's cry,
the boggart cautiously rocked the cot;
and the baby tried to grab his eye!

'He can see me!' he said. 'No, surely not.'
But the baby watched and showed no fear;
and the boggart had his great idea.
He would teach this boy magic, and use
   his trust
to live and grow strong on, as he must
unless he wanted to dwindle to dust.
So:
While the mother was busy
the boggart stayed with him.
For hours every day
he talked to him, played with him.
Never was baby so quiet and good.
If only his mother had understood!

The boggart brought him many things:
empty snail shells, sycamore wings,
scarlet rosehip, dandelion clock,
a wisp of wool from the upland flock,
a feather and an acorn cup
with honey in, for him to sup.
His mother threw them all away;
the boggart brought them back next day.

    And baby Joe learned and the boggart had fun.
    He did as he'd planned and he cared
       for none.

69

Part 4

You've surely seen cats turn and glare
suddenly, at empty air,
watch and follow with their stare
a silent Something passing by?
Something that your heavy eye
cannot see, will never see:
some thing – or is it some body!

That is how the boy would look,
lift his head from toy or book,
to gaze across the room awhile,
watching – Someone – with a smile.
Then he'd turn again to play.
His mother asked him, many a day,
what he saw. He'd never say.

Magic has its price. Young Joe
had learned to See, could not un-know.

In the day he'd See,
from the side of his eye,
strangest folk
go glimmering by,
laughing at him,

70

lovely and sly;
or shining coldly in the night
in their jack-o-lantern light. . .

'What are they? Fairies?' he asked in delight.
'Don't ever you call Them by that name!
They'd hear and They hate it!' the boggart
    said.
'I call 'em "Them Others".' He shook
    his head.
'I'd never name Them. Suppose They
    came!'

71

'But don't they grant wishes?' demanded
  Joe.
'Oh aye,' said the boggart, 'but when
  you'd got
whatever you wished for, boy, I know
you'd very soon wish that you had not!'

So Joe took warning and made no wishes,
not even to get out of doing the dishes.
But he had to go round Them whenever
  he saw Them.
He couldn't walk through Them, he
  couldn't ignore Them.

So if he was asked by some playmate,
'Why on earth don't you walk straight?'
What could he say?
'There's an elf in the way!'?
Or 'That's where a witch once cast a spell.'?
What would have happened? Can't you tell?

So everyone laughed at Dopey Joe;
and he dared not tell what they couldn't
  know.

His life was a burden when he went to
    school.
He made no friends – who'd be friends
    with a fool?
Enemies, yes, he had plenty of those:
he came home each day with a bleeding
    nose
or a blackened eye or stepped-on toes.
He never complained and he never wept,
but the boggart listened while he slept
and knew the bullies from Joe's dreaming
    mind.

Nobody's ever said boggarts are kind.

The boggart growled, 'If they do Joe harm,
I'll show them how a boggart can charm!
I'll not have my friend hurt. Let them
    beware!'
At last, the boggart had learned to care.

    His life was no longer a merry one:
    he couldn't say now that he cared
        for none.

After that, anyone picking on Joe
very quickly was filled with woe.
Their shoelaces loosened and tripped them
   up;
if they tried to drink, they dropped the cup;
they banged their elbows and squashed
   their thumbs,
their lunchtime sandwiches fell into
   crumbs,
their books got lost and their pencils broke;
and everyone else just thought it a joke!

Joe asked the boggart, 'Did you do all that?'
The boggart just grinned like a Cheshire
  cat.

'Now look here,' said Joe, 'they don't
  know why
these things happen to them; and I
couldn't explain to them if I would.
So you might as well stop it. You're
  doing no good.'

The boggart looked stubborn. 'Why don't
  you appear?'
Joe suggested. 'Let's show them you're
  here!'
'You reckon that seeing's believing? No,
believing is seeing,' the boggart told Joe.
'I can't appear. I tried with your ma.
She thought I was just a trick of the light;
and then when I tried again with your da,
he said there was summat wrong with
  his sight!
I guess folks used to hear and see
because they already believed in me.'

Part 5

'Joe,' said his father, 'haven't you got
a single friend?'
                         'No, Dad.'
                                     'Why not?'
'They hate me because I'm different, you
   know,'
Joe told him sadly. 'I'm like the white crow
that the other crows mob and drive away.
They'll even kill if it tries to stay.'

'Everyone's different in some way or other;
twins look alike, but not to their mother;
even peas in a pod aren't exactly the same,'
said his father, 'and "different" doesn't
   mean "shame".'

'Don't worry about it, Dad,' Joe said,
'All I really need is a different head!'

But things got no better in class or at play,
till Rob Dyson's gang, hunting Joe one day,
chased him home and he turned at bay
at the top of the lane. Rob raised his fist
and there was the boggart! He blew out
   a mist

and the lane was smoother than smoothest
  ice.
Rob's feet shot from under him; in a trice
he was slithering helplessly on his back,
sliding rapidly down the track.
All four of the other boys slipped and
  stumbled,
every one of them tripped and tumbled.

Rob got to his feet, gave Joe a glare:
'Watch it, Dopey! Don't you dare
trip us again. I'll make you pay.
Just wait and see! Tomorrow! Next day!'
He toppled again as he turned away.

Joe said doubtfully, 'Is it fair
to use a power they can't share?'
'Fair!' said the boggart. 'Tell me, Joe,
is five to one fair?'
               'We-ell,' Joe said. 'No.
OK, Boggart, set Rob free,
and hold the others still for me!'

Rob's gang staggered up, then fell again,
helpless to stay on their feet in the lane.
Rob stared at them, then scowled at Joe.
'Whatever's the matter? Do you know?'
Joe shrugged. 'It's magic, of course,' he said
and, grinning, ducked a smack on the head.

Joe bashed Rob and Rob bashed Joe,
    clumsily trading blow for blow.
Neither knew how to weave and bob,
So Rob thumped Joe and Joe thumped
    Rob.
At last, too tired to fight any more,
(and too bruised to want to) they stood
    toe to toe.
'Reckon we've just about evened the score,'
said Rob, breathing hard; and 'Yes!' gasped
    Joe.
'Friends?' asked Rob and 'Friends!' Joe
    breathed.
Behind them, the boggart invisibly seethed.

At last Joe had friends and the boggart
   found
when he looked for Joe, he was seldom
   around;
or he'd some excuse: 'Not this afternoon. . .'
'I can't come now. . .' 'I'll see you soon.'

The boggart grew jealous; and jealousy
   gnaws,
bitterly painful, whatever the cause.

So the boggart persisted. He got a cold
   stare:
'Oh, Boggart, I'm busy, do let me alone.
I can manage now perfectly well on my
   own.'
'Wouldn't you like to fly through the air
tonight?' coaxed the boggart. 'The
   broomstick's there!'

'I don't want your nasty old magic,' Joe
   cried.
'If you'd never taught me, I'm sure I'd
   have been
much better off!'
                'But you'd never have seen
Them Others dancing!' the boggart replied.

Joe thought of Them Others, uncannily
   fair,
the thrill of old magic when They were
   there. . .
'*Yes!* Better not know about fairies,' Joe
   lied.

And – Them Others came!
              He'd used That Name.

'Ach!' screamed the boggart. 'You're all
   alike,
you mortals, as dull as the mud in the dyke,
as thick as a plank and as stupid as stone!
I told you, you numbskull: LEAVE THAT
   NAME ALONE!'

And Joe lost his temper. He saw in a wink
Them Others watching as if at a play;
and at once he yelled, without stopping
    to think,
'I WISH YOU A THOUSAND YEARS
    AWAY!'

And before he even had time to blink
the boggart was gone.
                         'I won't do it again,
Boggart, come back!' Joe called, in vain.
'I didn't mean it!' But no-one replied.
Despairingly, Joe sat down and cried.

The boggart had warned him! Now Joe
    had got
what he had wished for – and wished
    he had not.
His boggart was gone for good: stuck fast
a thousand long years away in the past.

Part 6
Now this is the ancient tale folks tell,
of a boggart who seemed to be under a spell:

Long, long ago, there lived on a farm
a gentle old boggart. He did no harm:
and the farmers claimed he was under
    some charm.
For –
Whenever babies were born on that farm,
while their mothers were busy
the boggart would stay with them.
For hours every day
he would talk to them, play with them.
Never were babies so quiet and good.
The mothers valued him, as they should:
'A blessing upon you, Friend Boggart,'
    they'd say.
One of them will reward him some day.
Be it brounie or boggart, everyone knows,
if he is thanked with a gift of clothes,
he'll take them and vanish.
                    Where to? Who knows?
But now he's as free as the wind or the rain;
and no-one will ever see him again.

                                Ghillian Potts

COAT TALE

'Same colour,' said Tony standing there
At the Baths
With his wet hair plastered down:
His soup he meant and my cocoa –
Both the same shade of brown.
Brilliant though, after the swimming,
With the Chelsea buns we'd brought;
'Hey, I like your new anorak,' Tony said,
'Let's swap – go on, be a sport.'
'Just for the journey home,' I said,
And Tony said, 'OK.
When Mum gets paid she'll probably
Get me a new one, anyway.'
We dawdled home over Whitcliff
With the river below, way down,
And the town's spread out

All small and neat –
Just like a model of the town.
We were both pretty tired
But we talked a bit
And I told Tony a joke.
Then Tony said, 'My dad says
What he needs after swimming's
A smoke.'
I knew I was daft to say it but –
'My dad says your dad's a slave
To the fags.
If he keeps it up
He'll puff his way into his grave.'
When I said that, Tony went all red;
His temper blazed out straightaway:
'Oh, that's what your dad says
Is it, son?
Your dad's stupid, anyway.
He wants to mind his own business –
Just 'cos he gave up smoking himself!'
And he tore my coat off in his fury
And said,
'I'm chucking this over The Shelf!'
He flung my new blue anorak
Over Whitcliff's grassy edge
Where it's almost sheer – just halfway down

There's a crumbly sort of ledge.
We watched it flutter slowly away
Like some clumsy kind of bird;
Then I chucked Tony's after it;
I didn't speak a word.

Our tempers cooled pretty quickly
When we realized what we'd done.
Tony said, 'Blimey O'Reilly,
We're right up the creek now, son!'

85

We peered over the edge at the damage,
White-faced and feeling rotten,
The row we'd been having a minute ago
Forgotten.
Tony's old coat had caught in a bush
Growing out of a crack in the cliff;
It wasn't far down – we used a branch
And hooked it up in a jiff.
No way of getting my anorak though,
Caught on The Shelf, that had.
What would my mum say?
And my old man?
They'd both go raving mad!
Hopeless it looked;
I racked my brains
But couldn't think of a plan.
Tony, mooching along the edge, said,
'I think we can get it, man!'
He was standing where a tree came up –
Its roots were down on The Shelf;
'Get across to that tree,
Shin down to the ledge –
I think I can do it myself.'
'What do you do when you're down there?'
I said.
'How do you get to my blooming coat?

86

It's miles away along the ledge:
It'd need a mountain goat!'
'It's only about four yards along –
It might be only three.
Now don't go trying to put me off.
Help me get across to that tree.'
We needed something to bridge the gap –
A yard and a half, we thought;
We hunted about for branches:
All too rotten, or thin, or short.
Then I came up with a bright idea:
'Hey, the poles on the Forestry road!'
Tony caught on as quick as a flash:
'Hey yes, there should be a load!'
We knew they'd been felling trees there.
We dashed across in a tick:
Neatly trimmed poles,
Any thickness or length –
Tony just said, 'Take your pick!'
We carted back a good long one,
No way would it break or bend.
We got it up close to the edge
Of the cliff
And balanced it up on end.
The tree branched in a vee
At just the right height,

We judged overhangs of two feet.
We aimed it with care
Then we toppled the pole –
It dropped in the fork a treat.
Wedged tight, it was –
You could call it a bridge,
And Tony's preparing to cross;
He said, 'Over Niagara
On a greasy pole!
Hold this end firm will you, boss?'
In five steady steps
He crossed to the tree –
I nearly flipped my lid!
The drop was only a million feet.
He's got nerves of steel, that kid!
He was hugging the trunk
And in no time flat
He'd shinned down to the ledge below
And was inching along
With his back to the cliff –
About two yards to go.
My mouth and throat had gone all dry
But I peered down, lying flat,
At Tony squeezing along that ledge
Just wide enough for a cat.
There's one place

Where he's got to lean out
And duck under an awkward branch.
He slips –
There's a shower of stones –
He shouts,
'Just a minor avalanche!'
He's nearly there,
He's bending down,
He's got my anorak!
Where The Shelf's quite wide
He's putting it on:
He knows he can't carry it back.
Reverse trip harder
But he's back to the tree –
This time without a skid;
Gazes up at that pretty bare trunk,
Shouts,
'May have some problems here, kid!'
Scrabbles and scrambles
Up the trunk
Using every knob and lump;
Rests and mutters, 'Holy cow!
What do I hang on to now?'
Looking down, my heart goes cold –
Then I spot another hold;
He gains a branch – it's rather slender –

Not a breaker, just a bender;
Doesn't seem to share my fear,
Says,
'Wowee, the view from here!'
He climbs above the pole at last;
I say, 'Now this time,
Don't cross fast.'
He grins at me, wobbles across,
My anorak's all green with moss.

Tears in my eyes: just relief
That he's still in one piece –
More or less.
I go and hug him
Standing there,
A dusty, mossy mess.
He says, 'I wouldn't call
This coat of yours
Exactly fit to wear.
And I'll tell you something else, kid:
I was terrified down there!'

Eric Finney

MUD MICKEY
or The Pied Piper of Sandwell

Brunswick School's in Sandwell Borough,
By Albion's famous ground;
The M5 motorway, fast and wide,
Runs by its wall on the southern side;
A nicer school, to look at, you'd never find;
But let my story just unwind
And you will see the children suffering so
From teachers that your heart will melt –
On to this page your tears will flow!

Those teachers!
They shouted all day, then practised all
   night
On their husbands and wives
At making more miserable their pupils'
   lives.

91

They bit their heads off in their desks
And, however nicely they expressed
Their stories in Creative Writing
Or did their sums correctly, something
Was always wrong or not quite right.
(Though why these teachers were always
   angry
I'm not completely sure.
Perhaps it was something to do with their
   pay;
Or the way that Mr Barclay, the Head-
   master,
Made them stay till after six o'clock
To dust their classrooms or mount display
Each evening, and even, one Saturday,
Made them come in for a Staff Training
   Day
When Albion were playing Arsenal
In the quarter finals of the Cup.)

Anyway, enough of them for now.
Let's move on to the morning
That Mrs Carr, Class 6's teacher,
Rang in to say her temperature
Was in the hundreds and that unfortunately

She wasn't fit that day to rant and rave.
However, on the phone she gave
A list of things the class could do
And Mr Barclay sat in her desk,
Dispensing crosses and tiny ticks,
And generally looking severe and grave
To make quite sure the children didn't
    rave
It up or laugh or talk.
The class felt peeved.
When your teacher's away
You expect a different sort of day –
Pirates in the hall, a quiz,
Some easy sums, events not prominent
In Mr Barclay's scheme of things.
The class felt peeved,
But most especially the boy
Who sat right next to teacher's desk
    because,
As you might guess, he was
The one who Mrs Carr liked least
And picked on when her beast-
ly temper got the better of her.
His name was Mickey. Our hero.
Mickey. Our story's his.

But after dinner, when Class 6
Came grumbling back into their places,
Another teacher sat behind the desk,
A ragged sort of fellow with long hair
That hadn't seen a comb for years.
He wore no tie and took no care
With shoes or shirts. He made them face
The front and called the register,
Not even blinking when Martin Simpson
Twice called him 'Miss' by error,
And Erica Young stuck out her tongue
And Clive told on her at the top of his voice.
The new teacher spread his arms out wide.
'Tell-tales are for nurseries,' he sighed.
'Class Six, you've got a choice.
Behave yourselves or go to bed tonight
With a helluva headache, for I've a helluva
    voice
On me as well as Clive. You choose.
I flit around from school to school
So it doesn't make much difference to me
If you spend your afternoon in misery.
Tomorrow I'll be gone and far away,
Teaching at Albion Primary.'
He turned and glanced towards the board,
Then wiped off all of Mr Barclay's work.

'I've something better for you shower
To get us through the next couple of
      hours.'
He rummaged in his bag to find a book,
Then held it up and showed the cover.
'As you'll soon find, I'm a poetry lover.
In here's a poem by Robert Browning
That's called *The Pied Piper of Hamelin*.
What's it about? About rats and children,
Mean adults and the Piper's revenge on
      them;
About how he piped away a horde of rats,
And when the grown-ups wouldn't pay up,
Piped their children away to a happier land.
So get yourselves comfortable to listen!
Pin back your ears or I'll pin them back
      for you!
Don't move an inch or you'll feel the
      rat's pinch!
Move a foot – and you'll feel *my* boot!'
He found his place and began to read.

'Hamelin Town's in Brunswick,
By famous Hanover city;
The river Weser, deep and wide,
Washes its wall on the southern side;

A pleasanter spot you never spied;
But, when begins my ditty,
Almost five hundred years ago,
To see the townsfolk suffer so
From vermin, was a pity.'

'Our school's called Brunswick!' Sophie
    calls.
'What's vermin, sir?' the cheeky Mickey
    bawls.
'Are teachers vermin?' He turns and grins
    for applause.
'Rats!' the strange teacher says. 'That's
    what they are.
Still – teachers, rats! There's sometimes not
Much difference between them in my
    experience!
Now settle down, you idle lot. *Rats!*
They fought the dogs and killed the cats,
And bit the babies in their cradles. . .'

'What's your name, sir?' our Mickey asks.
The teacher laughs. 'It's Piper, Mr Piper.
You have been warned!' he says as Mickey
    gasps.

*

Next morning Mickey wakes to pouring
    rain.
It's running down the windowpane
And gurgling through the drains and
    gutters.
Outside the world's awash with water,
Enough to make you feel like Noah.
Then Mickey remembers it's Friday, games
    day,
And Mrs Carr is back today. And it's
    raining
On games day. His tummy sinks.

'Mum, I'm poorly. My forehead's boiling
    hot.
Look at my tongue. It's covered with
    spots.'
Mum lowers her paper to look at the tongue
That he thrusts in her face for closer
    inspection.
'Take an aspirin, Mickey. You'll soon be
    fine.

Do you want money for dinner? Look
  in my purse.
Is that the time? I've got to run.
And remember – *be good at school today
  for Mrs Carr!*
Oh, by the way, what's this I found
Floating around in your trouser pocket?
  A poem?
  Mrs Carr was born in a jar.
  Mrs Carr has got catarrh.
I think you'd better throw that away!'

Be good at school! For Mickey that's hard
  enough
At the best of times, but a day like this
  it's tough-
er than usual. Any day with Mrs Carr
  is rough,
But a games–less Friday would give the
  SAS the shivers.
On the way to school the roads are rivers,
The birds are using the trees as enormous
  umbrellas;
Complete with seagulls the field's a lake.

It's weather to break a footballer's heart!
'Games, Mickey?' says Mrs Carr. She
　　blows her nose.
'You dozy boy! There isn't a chance.
Now, for goodness sake, don't dance
Around my desk. Sit down and read a
　　book.'
She gives the board a startled glance.
'What drivel's this? *The Pied Piper of
　　Hamelin?*'
'It's a poem by Robert Browning,'
Says Mickey, suddenly remembering
That Mr Piper who made him laugh.
'He piped the children away into a happier
　　land
Through a hole in the hill because he
　　couldn't stand
The way the grown-ups treated him.'
'A happier land?' his teacher snaps.
'What rubbish! Class 6 – put your hands
　　in your laps!'
She wipes the blackboard and now he's
　　gone,
Except in memory, that funny man
Who read them the poem.

Assembly at nine, hymn practice half-past.
The piano's out of tune, the choir even
    worse.
Mr Barclay's office after – a terrible to-do.
'You interrupted Mr Peters? You threw
    a shoe?
Mickey! Two thousand lines for you!'
Playtime's inside. It's followed by maths.
Mrs Carr's in a temper more terrible than
    usual.
It's 'Mickey, do this!' and 'Mickey, do that!
Can't you hurry? Be neater? Be quieter?
    Behave?'
Mickey eyes the window as the teacher
    raves,
For the storm is easing off, the rain is
    dying away.
Mrs Carr: 'No dinner, Mickey, till that
    work is done.
In the corner's where you belong.'
Thinks Mickey: maybe the safest place
    to be!
He asks again, though the answer's sure
    to be 'No',
'Games, Mrs Carr? Can't we give it a go?'

'In this weather?' she shouts. 'Don't be
    utterly stupid!
I forbid you to ask that question again.
And what did you do for that teacher
    yesterday?
Listened to poems? Wrote verses of your
    own?
Good lord! You might as well have stayed
    at home.'
Mickey feels in his pocket. His poem's
    still there.
He'd love to read it out. He wouldn't care
What Mrs Carr thought.

Then – at long last – the morning's over.
The children close their books and fold
    their arms.
They file in silence, even Mickey, out
    of harm's
Way past Mrs Carr who frowns and
    shakes her head
And wishes she'd never got out of bed.
They file into the hall and look and wait –
And sigh. The trays of food look awful,

The peas like bullets, the mash full of
    lumps,
The beef like pumps from the Lost Property
    Box
That mice have chewed over and cook has
    braised.
Over it all Mrs Barrow's religiously ladled
A blanket of oozing, nutritious brown
    stew.
For pudding it's shortcake so hard it would
    make
The teeth of a road drill crumble and ache!

Mickey inspects it from the queue.
'Needs banning!' he moans, as well might
    you.
'Needs banning!' he says more loudly
As he picks up his tray and makes for
    his place.

The dinner ladies hear and gather round.
Like avenging vultures they stand by his
    table,
Mrs Postones, Mrs Smithson, Mrs Patton,
    Mrs Lear.
'Our Mickey's in a mood. It's trouble
    he's after,'
They mutter. 'Mickey! Eat it now.
We don't want some terrible row.
Come on, Mickey. You'll make us late,
So stop inside or clean your plate!'

Mickey stands it so long, then something
    snaps.
The Pied Piper wouldn't have put up with
    this,
Nor that teacher from yesterday, Mr Piper.
He'd have told them what to do
With their awful, inedible meal.
He clambers to his feet and pushes back
    his plate.
'Hey! Where you going?' calls Dennis,
    his mate.
'You're not finished! Wait!'
'I've had enough,' says Mickey. 'I've had
    my fill.'

103

He crosses to the hatch and calls across
  the till,
'Mrs Barrow!' Cook's head turns. 'Yes,
  luv?'
Seconds? For Mickey? She beams with
  pride.
Mickey wonders – he might be making
  a mistake –
But doesn't wonder long. He has his pride
  too.
'Mrs Barrow – ' 'Yes, luv.' 'I'm sorry,
  Mrs Barrow.
I hate this meal. I want my money back.'

Round the hall the cook's agonised cry
  reverberates.
Every jaw stops chewing. Instantly.
Even Robert, the slowest eater in the world,
Listens between chomps. The cutlery
  rattles.
The teacher on duty raises her head.
'What's on fire? What's happening?' she
  says.
But cook's nose is turning a murderous
  purple.

'Happening – ?' Words fail Mrs Barrow.
Her hand is reaching for her heaviest ladle.
'Wait!' the teacher shouts, up-ending her
   chair.
The ladle wavers and wavers in the air,
Then suddenly the cook grabs hold of
   Mickey's hair.
Quick as a laser the teacher flies across
   the hall.
'Mickey! By my desk! I'll deal with you
   later.'
'But Miss – ' 'Mickey, I'm warning you!'
The ladle comes down. The slop bowl flies.
'He asked for his money back! That's what's
   the matter!'

Downstairs is lonely. Mickey's fed up.
Who'd have thought that speaking the truth
Would lead to a punch-up?
Be frank, stand straight and speak your
  mind
Adults tell you all the time.
It isn't kind if they don't mean what
  they say.
He opens the door and pops his head
  outside.
The rain has stopped, the sun's begun
  to shine.
The watery field beckons. 'Come out!'
  it whispers.
But Mrs Lear is coming down the stairs,
Shepherding infants to put their coats on.
'Come back in and go where teacher put
  you!
Stand by the desk and face the music.
It's time you learnt that life's no picnic.'
He nearly obeys. But suddenly a calm
Feeling of knowing exactly what to do
Comes over him. He whirls
And takes the closest infant's arm.
'Come on!' he calls to the startled line
Of five-year-old faces. 'No need for coats!'

106

He leads them out into the steaming yard.
'Come on!' he calls. 'You won't come
  to harm!'
'Stop stop stop!' the ladies call,
But it's far too late. In pairs, and hand in hand,
The thirty infants toddle down the bank.
They plunge on to the field,
And jump into the double-creamy mud.
It's mud that's fit for pigs,
Still churned by last Friday's match,
Furrows ploughed by a hundred boots
And filled to overflowing
By ankle-deep puddles you could paddle
  a canoe in.

The infants avoid the dinner ladies' eyes
And Mickey laughs. 'Play in it!' he yells.
'Roll in it! Throw it! Play piggy-back in it!
Make mud-pies! Eat it! Do what you like!
I don't care!'

'Come back! Come back!' the dinner ladies
   call
From the dividing line between mud and
   playground.
'Careful, Jeremy. You're going to fall!
The mess you're getting in! The mess!
   The mess!'
But no-one's coming back and more are
   piling in.
The rest of the infants stream out through
   the doors,
See what's happening, run past the
   grown-ups'
Outstretched hands and jump into the mud.
The juniors too have finished dinner
(Or, rather, left it) and are wading in.
Mrs Postones bravely slithers
Down the bank, slips and a moment later's

Completely splattered from head to toe.
'Where's Mickey?' the dinner ladies bawl.
'It's his fault! He started it all!'
'Come on!' shouts Mickey. 'All in line.'
At the front he blows an imaginary pipe.

'What's happening out there?' Mrs Carr
    asks,
Half-asleep in the staffroom, feet up on
    the table.
'That noise in the playground. It sounds
    like a battle.'
Mr Peters rustles his morning paper.
'Nothing to do with us till playtime's over.
I haven't recovered from assembly yet.'
Mrs Cope, the deputy, pulls back the nets.
She stares a long moment, then lets them
    flop.
Her face is aghast, a mask of horror.
'It's a riot. It's chaos. They're running
    amok.
The children are doing the conga across
    the field.
There's a lad in the front all covered in mud,

From your class, Ethel, your shoe-
    throwing friend.'
'Mickey?' His teacher jumps to her feet
And darts to the window. She stares in
    horror –
'I don't believe it! I can't! I won't!'
For outside there's a monstrous sight,
Three hundred children, plastered head to
    toe,
Dancing and jiving, slithering and sliding.
At the head of them's Mickey, that
    well-known demon,
Splitting his face a grin like a melon.

Mud's dripping from his chin,
Mud's running from his hair,
Mud's oozing through his toes.
It's coming out of his ears,
It's coming out of his nose.
'*Mickey!*' Mrs Carr bawls. '*Stop, boy!*'

Around the school the houses rattle,
Windows, doorframes, chimneys shiver.
In number 70 a baby starts to cry;
In 24 a night-worker dreams a battle
Is raging through his belovèd front garden.
And on the road below the school
An ancient car, a psychedelic Beetle,
En route from Albion to Hallam Junior,
Comes screeching to a sudden halt.
'Mickey?' thinks Mr Piper. 'I remember
    now.
Brunswick School! That's where I left my
    book!'
He signals right. His Beetle lumbers up the
drive.

On the field poor Mickey's stumbled to
    a halt.
The mud-drenched line behind him's
    stopped its singing.
'*Mickey!*' Mrs Carr bellows. '*Come here
at once!*'
But up the drive the Beetle's chugging.
The driver beeps his horn and winds his
    window down.

'Just passing,' Mr Piper waves and calls.
He clambers from his car and stretches.
'My, my!' he says. 'You lot are muddy!
Class 6! That's you beneath that muck?'
  He laughs.
'I think I left my book on teacher's desk.'
'That's Mr Piper,' the deputy tells Mrs
  Carr.
'The children loved him.'
'Loved him?' says Mrs Carr. She leans
  right out.
'I saw the things you made my children
  write,'
She shouts. 'It isn't good enough.
You go and take your poetry with you.'
She chucks the book. The book flies
  through the air
And lands, spine broken, leaves muddied,
  cover torn,

At Mr Piper's feet, a perfect aim.
'The happier land?' pleads Mickey from
   the mud.
'Where is it, Mr Piper? Tell us, please!'
'I loved that book!' shouts Mr Piper,
   'You've got me angry!'
He jumps back in his car and toots his horn.
'The happier land? We'll find it, Mickey!
   Follow me!'
The children follow. The line begins to
   dance.

And the last that was seen of that conga,
It was heading due south
In search of the happier land,
Children followed by dinner ladies,
Followed by teachers, stumbling and
   pleading,
Followed by the Head in his Honda,

Woken from a snooze in his study
To find his school missing.
As the shadows lengthen
Its trail grows weaker, not stronger.
'A missing school? Have you seen a
    missing school?
Perhaps it's passed your house?'

Perhaps. Or perhaps they've already found
    the happier land
(And was Mr Piper really the Piper?).

Brunswick School's in Sandwell Borough,
By Albion's famous ground;
The M5 motorway, fast and wide,
Runs by its wall on the southern side;
A nicer school, to look at, you'd never find;
Except that now a sign
Says CLOSED FOR EVER, grass binds
Its fingers round the playground tarmac,
The wind
Whistles through its empty rooms,
And the ghost of a pupil left behind
Peers through Mr Barclay's flip-flapping blind.

Brian Morse

CAT ON THE ROOF

'Puss, Puss.'

'Oh, Jennifer, please, don't make such
   a fuss;
Cat out of sight for less than a minute
And you think that some scoundrel
Has trapped it to skin it.'

'Oh Mother, it's up on the top of the wall.'

'Well, why are you worrying?
Cats don't fall.'

'But it's only a kitten.'

And Puss jumped on the edge
Of the crumbling brick of the
   back window-ledge.

'Oh, mother, look now.
It's climbing the tiles.'

And they watched as it crept
To the ridge of the roof,
Then suddenly swept
With lithe, feline grace
To a perilous spot at the chimney-pot base.
Sure-footed it circled and boldly stared
   round;
Then the clown
Suddenly knew that it couldn't get down.

And Gran tossed her head
And sniffed and then said,
'Serve it jolly well right
For getting itself in this dangerous plight.
Leave it up there all day –
Even better, all night.'

116

But Jennifer wailed
And her mother alone
Kept her calm.
She dashed off indoors to get on the phone.
And Grandfather left off his work in the
    shed,
And Father, when phoned,
Said he wished it was dead.
But he got in his car
And organized men
Collecting some ladders;
They reared them up then
To lean on the gutter.

Father climbed first
And lay on the slope
Of the roof
With an armful and fistful
Of tightly coiled rope.
Then Grandfather carefully climbed up his
    back
And quietly prayed that the roof wouldn't
    crack.

Then Johnny next door –
He's fifteen or so –
Clambered up Father
And Grandfather too;
By pulling with fingers
And digging with toes
He reached to the chimney.

Then up to the ladder the vicar's child
    stepped;
Over Father, Grandfather and Johnny
He crept
And, holding the ridge with one hand,
Reached out for the cat
Which suddenly crouched and
Terrified,
Leapt
To his head,
To the ridge,
To the tiles – then he fled
To Johnny,
To Grandfather's shoulders,
To Father's broad back,
And then scampered off inside the roof
    gutter,

Then sprang to a tree,
To a bush,
To the ground.

So Grandma swung round
With a furious mutter.
'I should think they're all mad;
What a game to be at,
And all for the sake of that lunatic cat.'

Then Grandma – no nonsense –
With her hand to her eye
Because of the glare from the blue of
   the sky,
Shouted into the light,
'Come on down now, my lad.'

But the vicar's young boy
Couldn't move;
His fingers were tight,
And he lay by the chimney-stack
Stiffened with fright.

So Johnny talked softly,
And Grandfather called,
But the boy wouldn't move;

And Father, with elbow jammed tight
  in a groove,
Shouted,
'Peter, hold tight!
When my elbow is free I think that we
  might. . .'

But Grandmother muttering,
'Idiot cat,'
Hitched up her skirts and snatched off
  her hat,
Then mounted the ladder,
Dug heels into Father,
Trod on Grandfather's face
Knelt over Johnny
And at last got a place
Alongside young Peter.

'Young Peter, I'm Grandma;
A nice thing, must say,
Crawling up on a roof
At my time of day.'

And she pulled him up close
In the comforting band
Of her skinny old arm.

120

The blue veins lay thick
On the bones of her hand.

'And I'll tell you this, boy,'
She said with a frown,
'I got right up here
But I can't scramble down;
My glasses, you know, bi-focals – all
    blurred;
Now, get me down, boy.'

They clung to each other
And then Peter stirred.
He lay on his side
With his cheek on a tile,
And he looked up at Gran
With a white little smile.
And they groped with their feet
And found Johnny's head,
And scraped down his ears
For a safe place to tread;
And Grandmother's foot slid from Johnny's
    new coat
And found a good ledge on Grandfather's
    throat;
And then both took a stand
On the broad, fleshy platform of Father's
    big hand.

Then both down the ladder,
Peter inside,
Moved lower and lower
With only the sound
Of Grandmother's hands on the wood
    as they slide;
And at last both her feet
Are down flat on the ground.

122

Then Johnny,
Grandfather,
And Father
Climbed down,
And Mother served tea;
And Grandmother, carefully dusting her
    gown,
Said firmly,
'Well, now that I'm down,
You can put in a measure of brandy for me.'

She sat on the step
With her feet on the mat,
And leaned back her head
And then suddenly said
(You might almost say 'spat'),

'That stupid and irresponsible cat,
That brainless and feckless and cretinous
    pest –
I shall have to go soon and take a long rest –
That pin-headed, dense, irrepressible
    beast. . .'

123

Grandma paused,
And Jennifer thought
That as it was hers
Perhaps that she ought,
At the least,
To say she was sorry
For the trouble she'd caused. . .

'What was that?
Sorry?'
Grandmother gasped.
'And what if it ran off in front of a lorry?
Say sorry?!
With five wretched people squashed flat
For the sake of one useless, malevolent cat?

Come on, now, young Peter,
You'd best get our hats
And walk me inside. . .
I'm not very fond, you may guess, boy,
Of cats.'

Gregory Harrison

THE OLD DUPPY'S CURSE
Or How I Was Turned into a Crocodile!

Part One

'If you walk through a puddle,
You'll get into trouble,'
My mother said to me.
When I asked her, 'Why?'
She said with a sigh,
'Because I said so! See!'

But that night in bed,
I hugged Mum and said,
'If I ask you something, don't shout.
It's just that this morning
You gave me a warning.
Please tell me what that was about.

125

I still do not get
Why my socks can't get wet.'
Mum said, 'Jean, it's something much
    worse.
It's something so evil
It's hard to believe. . .
It's the fault of the old duppy's curse.

See, when I was nine,
I thought it was fine
When off to see Gran I was sent.
She gave us the airfare,
Told us how to get there,
So off to Barbados we went!

It's a very sad story
And one that I'm sorry
To say has just me to blame.
For by my gran's barn
And causing no harm
Lived a duppy, with eyes of red flame.'

'A duppy? What's that?
A fish or a cat?
My! What a peculiar word!
It sounds so absurd.

A word I've not heard.
Is it mineral, veggie or bird?'

'Duppies are ghosts
That stay with their hosts
And scare all the neighbours away.
They say to be free
That water's the key,
It's water that keeps them at bay.

So one night I sneaked out,
There was no-one about,
And the moon was up high in the sky.
I went to our well
(It's a sad tale to tell,
But I'm not going to tell you a lie).

I filled up my pail,
Sure that I couldn't fail,
And up to the barn on tiptoe
I silently crept.
As the poor duppy slept
I circled him, silent and slow.

Over the duppy
I then held my bucket

And with a great flourish I said,
"Mr Duppy – it's me!
You are now history!"
And I dumped the whole lot on his head!

The furious duppy
Rose up high above me
And pointing his finger he growled,
"As you're so fond of water,
When you have a daughter. . ."
He paused as the wind moaned and howled.

"When you have a child,
Of her you'll be proud,
But she'd better stay out of the rain. . .
If she goes through a puddle
She'll be in BIG trouble,
And you'll be the person to blame.

Her face will start changing,
Her limbs rearranging,
She'll change right before you, and then,
You won't recognize her.
In fact you'll despise her.
And you won't see her true face again. . ."

And that is why, Jean,
It's not me being mean,
Please believe what I'm saying to you.
You mustn't go wading,
Or else I'm afraid
That the old duppy's curse will come true.'

Then Mum tucked me in,
Kissed my forehead, my chin.
And she patted my hands and my head.
She switched off my light,
Saying, 'Sleep well. Good-night.'
But I dreamt of the duppy instead,
And the horrible things he had said.

Part Two

The very next day, it rained and it poured,
All day I'd been sitting down, terribly
  bored.
So when Mum arrived to get me from
  school,
I thought to myself, 'I shall test out
  Mum's rule!'

Deep down I had thought that my mum'd
  been joking,
So I danced along till Mum called me
  provoking.
I came to a puddle; before she could stop
  me,
I waded right through it – and that's
  when it shocked me. . .

When I'd started to wade, I had shoes
  on my feet.
And my socks were pulled up – all tidy
  and neat.
But when I came out, instead of each shoe,
I had massive CLAWS – it's perfectly true!

130

My teeth seemed to sprout from all over
   my head,
And as for my nose! What more can be said?
I looked in the puddle. I just couldn't smile.
There! My reflection! A huge crocodile!

I could see my reflection there in the water.
My body was fatter, more wrinkled and
   shorter.
My nostrils seemed metres away from
   my eyes,
And my teeth were a huge and inelegant
   size.

Gone was my beautiful brown and soft
   skin.
I'd knobbles without, and a tough hide
   within.
From out of my back I now grew a tail.
I wanted to howl and to shriek and to wail.

For I had been warned. Yes, I had been told.
But I thought I was clever. I thought
   I was bold.
And into the puddle I'd wanted to splash.

Now all I could do was to watch people
  dash
To the left and the right of me. No-one
  would stay.
With cries of '*Get going!*' and '*Help!*' and
  '*Gangway!*'

I shouted, 'Do something, Mum! Now!
  Do it quick!'
So she did. She said, 'Jean, serves you
  right – you're so thick!'
With her hands on her hips she said,
  'What did I say?
Suppose I can't help you and you're stuck
  that way?'

Mum was annoyed – that was quite plain
  to see.
I thought to myself, Well, what about me!
Mum said with a frown, 'We'd better
  get home.
And when we get there, I'll get on the
  phone
And phone up Great-granny who lives
  on a farm
Away in Barbados. She'll help. There's
  no harm

In trying at any rate. Jean, you're so wild!
You're an exasperating,

IRRITATING
AGGRAVATING,
child!'

Mum said, 'Great-gran's wise and she'll
  help us for sure.
It's guaranteed that she can tell us the cure.
You've got to get home, Jean, that's what
  you must do,
Or else you may end up on show in a zoo.'
'It's not fair! I'm not moving,' I started
  to moan.
'Mum, couldn't you lift me and carry
  me home?'

Mum looked at me, scratched an ear,
  blinked an eye.
'You've got to be joking, Jean!' came
  her reply.
'But don't worry, darling, the duppy told
  lies.
Of course I still love you – in spite of
  your size!'

133

NEE! NAA! NEE! NAA! The sound filled
  my head.
Why wasn't I changed to a rabbit instead?

'Oh Mum! Oh Mum! I can hear sirens
  wailing,'
I cried, my tail thrashing and threshing
  and flailing.
Above us a chopper, its rotor-blades
  humming,
Called out on its speaker, 'Don't panic!
  We're coming!'

'Run, Jean! You're short but there's no-one
    to match you!
For goodness sake, darling, please don't
    let them catch you!'
'I can't just go waddling right down the
    High Street!'
I said. 'What about all the people I'll meet?'

'We'll have to split up, we're too easy
    to spot.
They'll all think you'll eat me, as likely
    as not,'
Said my mum.
'Right!' I said. 'First, I'll get off this street.
I'll get home on my own two – or rather
    – four feet.

Mum, head off home and I'll be right
    behind you.'
'OK, Jean,' Mum said. 'But please don't
    let them find you.'
I ducked round a corner and tucked in
    my bum,
Whilst the chopper above me continued
    to hum.

What could I do? Would I ever get home?
Never before had I felt so alone.
So afraid and so positive that I'd be spied.
There aren't many places a big croc can
    hide.

By some smelly old bins I ran into a cat.
It snarled, arched its back, bared its teeth
    and then spat.
A girl wearing glasses stepped right on
    my tail.
I started to howl and she started to wail.
I headed for home just as fast as I could.
(I shouldn't have bothered, it did little
    good!)

A man who was out with his dog had a fit.
I don't think he liked me – not one little bit.
He shivered, he quivered, he screamed
and he shook.
And all of my powers of persuasion it took,
To convince with my biggest and beamiest
smile
That I would *not* eat him. Not this
crocodile!

I met with a team from the Six O'Clock
News.
'You'll make a great wallet or a new
pair of shoes!'
Said the journalist to me, but I'd had
enough.
As if I would listen all day to such stuff!

The clouds had stopped raining. The sun
had come out.
The streets were deserted, no-one was
about.

At last I reached home. I hadn't been
    skiving,
But it still took an hour of ducking and
    diving.
For scorning Mum's warning, I felt such
    a twerp!
And being a reptile was *really* hard work!

Sam from next door came out and he
    saw me.
He called out, 'Mum! Mum! There's a
    crocodile. Look! See!'
Hands on her hips, her eyes wide with
    surprise,
She said, 'Samuel Wells! Don't you dare
    tell such lies.'

His mum wagged her finger and told
    him off more,
And just when I thought that she'd see
    me for sure
And scream, yell or chuck things or faint
    on the floor,
My mum heard the racket and opened
    our door.

Part Three

'Hello there, Great-Grandma!' I called
   down the phone.
Mum shook her head and she started to
   moan.
'Don't shout in her ear, Jean! I'm deaf
   now! Good gracious!
Are you trying to yell all the way to
   Barbados?'

'Hello mi dear! Mi fav'rite gran-chile!'
Said Great-granny. 'I hear that you're a
   . . . crocodile.'
'Oh, yes I am, Gran, and I want to
   change back.
So please tell me how I should start to
   do that.'
'We're stuck, Gran,' Mum said, 'that's
   why we called you.
Please help – 'cause we don't have a clue
   what to do!'

139

'Well, how did the poor gal get into this
    muddle?
You didn't allow her to wade through
    a puddle?'
'You've got it in one, Gran!' my mum
    shouted out.
'That's it in a nutshell, that's what it's
    about!'
'Ah! The old duppy's curse. So *that's*
    what's going on.
I'll check in my fact book. Wait there.
    Won't be long.'

'But Gran, we can't wait. The police are
    outside,'
Said my mum.
'Sorry, dear. Then you'll just have to hide.
I'll find out the cure just as soon as I'm able.
Till then, try the wardrobe or under the
    table.'
I shivered and shook, from my tail to
    my ears,
Whilst down from my eyes fell huge
    crocodile tears.
        (Real ones!)

Meanwhile, outside the house. . .

'This is the police. We are here on all sides.
We know you are in there, so don't try
    to hide.
Come out right this second. I've got lots
    of men.
Or we're coming in – I won't say it again!'

'Do hurry up, Gran. . . ' Mum said to
    the phone.
But the silence that answered showed we
    were alone.
'Please, Mum! Do something!' I shrieked
    in her ear.
'I'm trying to, darling. You just stay right
    there.'

'Hello? Can you hear me? Where's everyone
    gone?'
Mum gave a sigh as Gran yelled down
    the phone.
'We thought you'd got lost, Gran.' Mum
    pulled up a seat.
And what Granny said, well I just can't
    repeat!

'If my heart should fail, Gran, it's all
  on your head.
Speak a bit faster – *please*!' That's what
  Mum said.
'Umm-hhmm. . . Yeah. . . Yeah. . . Oh,
  I see. . .
What . . . ? Are you sure. . . ? Why next
  to a tree. . . ?
Umm. . . Yep. . . Oh, I understand. . .
I just hope this works, 'cause it sounds
  a weird plan. . .

Of course I believe you. No, I didn't say. . .
All right, Gran. . . all right, dear. . . Well,
  have it your way.
I'll phone you back after and tell you
  the worst.
But we've got to go off now and try
  it out first.
Gran, you're a marvel! An angel! A brick!
But goodness to gracious, you get the
  hump quick!'

'What is it?' I asked her, 'I'm bursting
  to know.'
'Wait!' Mum said. 'Be quiet and keep
  your voice low.'
So we ran through the kitchen, afraid
  who we'd meet.
(My nose was so low, I tripped over
  my feet.)
Mum said, 'Keep your eyes peeled and
  say if you see
A glistening puddle not far from a tree.'

We walked round the garden. I found
   one at last.
'Here's one, Mum, but hurry. It's drying
   up fast.'
'OK, Jean. Now you've got to walk
   backwards through it.
Don't stand there and argue. Get moving!
   Just do it!
It's got to be now, Jean. It's now or
   it's never.
Or else you may well be a reptile for ever.'

So I shut my eyes tight and I did as
   Mum said.
My tail disappeared. Back came my true
   head.
Two legs and two arms. And small,
   discrete teeth.
No knobbly bits with a tough hide beneath.
Mum hugged me. I looked up at her
   and I said,
'The next time it's raining, I'm staying
   in bed!'

Malorie Blackman

BENNY McEEVER

Benny McEever
Two left feet
Lived in a council house
On Poverty Street.
Never knew his mother
His dad was on the rocks
Lived down the Embankment
In a cardboard box.
His gran once told him
She'd seen him around
Playing a cornet for pennies
Down the Underground.
Benny McEever
Holes in his shoes
Never lost nothing
Nothing to lose

'Cept a mouthpiece off a cornet
Had once been his dad's
That his grandmother found one day
And gave to the lad.
And Benny learned to play it
Played mournful and sad
Melodies about the love
Poor Benny never had.

Dirty-neck Benny
Brillo-pad hair
Wore a sign on his face
Said, 'I don't care.'
Benny had a heart
Like a dried-up well
Love was a word
He never learned to spell.
His school said Benny
Was a real dead loss
His brain was stuffed

With candy floss.
Kids moved aside
To let him pass
He sat on his own
At the back of the class.

Started playing truant
Wandered all alone
Aimless and friendless
All around the town.
Walked into a jewellery shop
Saw a gold watch there
Slipped it in his pocket
Ran out into the square.
Back in the schoolyard
The whisper went round,
'Seen Benny's watch?
Cost two hundred pound!
Where d'you get it, Benny?'
They all asked jealously
And proudly Benny answered,
'My dad bought it me.'
He hadn't really meant it
The lie had been a game
But the more he repeated it
The truer it became.

When Benny ran home
His gran was outside
With two tall policemen
Standing by her side.
And Benny started running
The wind in his hair
Through back yards and alleyways
It didn't matter where.
Fear screamed inside his skull
He felt his wild heart beat
And always behind him
The sound of running feet.
He dashed through the market
Dodging in and out
And the air was filled with whistling
Sirens and shouts.
At last behind the roller rink
He fell to the floor
Poor Benny McEever
Couldn't run any more.

In front of the magistrate
Hangdog Billy stood.
The social worker told the court,
'It must be in his blood.
His mother wasn't any good
His father was the same.
If you ask me, Your Honour,
Heredity's to blame.'

'I just can't control him,'
His grandmother said.
'Won't do anything I say
Just lies all day in bed.'

Benny in a special school
Lost and alone
Felt his heart turning
Into a stone.
He took out the mouthpiece
That he kept on a string
Pressed it softly to his lips
And made the metal sing.
It sang a song of heartbreak
That made the sad stars weep
Till finally, still playing,
Benny fell asleep.

Then one day Benny
Went walking by the shore
Past cranes and ships and dockyards
Where he'd never walked before.
Heard footsteps close behind him
Strange voices everywhere
But when Benny turned to look around
Nobody was there.
Benny stood frozen
Heard the seagull's cries
While the sea mist descended
Like a scarf about his eyes.
Benny running blindly
Down Dead End Lane
Heard a voice whispering
Benny's own name.
'Benny McEever
There's nothing to fear.
Come on up, Benny,
I'm waiting for you here.'

Better run, Benny,
You'd better beware
But everywhere that Benny ran
The voice was always there.

Found his feet walking
Up stairs, across a floor
Found his hand turning
The handle of a door.
And the voice spoke softly
Cutting Benny like a knife,

'I've been waiting for you, Benny,
The whole of our life.'
Benny saw a figure
Sitting all alone
Face as old as Charity
Eyes like stone.
His boots let water
His coat was a sack
His hands were bent and buckled
His fingernails black.
He called Benny over
The soft voice was sad.
He said,
'I want to tell you, Benny
All about your dad.
I knew him well, Benny.'
And the old man's eyes were calm.
'I was closer to your father
Than my own right arm.
It was only bad luck
That led him astray
He was never as bad
As people might say.'

Then he took out a bundle
And said with a sigh,
'*Your dad sent you this
To remember him by.*'
Benny's nervous fingers
Untied the string.
He found a battered trumpet
Lying there within.
He stuck on the mouthpiece
Blew strong and bold
And the sweet notes cascaded
Like a shower of gold.

'*Tell my dad. . .* ' said Benny
But nobody was there
Just a door swinging slowly,
The room quite bare.

And Benny strode out
Past the cranes and the ships
His dad's battered cornet
Pressed to his lips.
And a host of children
Skipped after the boy
Their voices raised high
In an anthem of joy.
And the song they sang
Soared sweet and high
Blowing like a tempest
Across the sky.
It screamed through the schoolroom
It roared through the port
It scattered the papers
In the magistrates court.
And Benny remembered
His whole life long.
How one great Good
Could drive out every Wrong.

Gareth Owen

THE PIRATE BABY

Well, me hearties, now I'll tell 'ee
  Such a tale of pirates bold!
Rich and tangy from the salt sea,
  All shot through with gleams of gold.

What a tale of sound and fury!
  There be fighting, blood and gore!
Clang of cutlass, bang of cannons!
  Treasure piled up, and what's more. . .

Heaps of nappies, rows of bottles,
  Most for milk and not for rum,
And a pair of pirate captains
  Who become a dad, and mum.

155

Both of them were very famous;
  One, a lady whose dread name
Filled men's hearts with fear and panic
  All along the Spanish Main.

Keel-haul Annie was that woman,
  She had sunk a thousand ships;
Kept her filthy crew obedient
  With loud curses (and a whip).

Annie was a mighty woman,
  Tough and tall and very strong.
Always carried two big pistols
  And a cutlass, four feet long.

Just as scary was the other
  Pirate who could make hearts freeze;
Cut-throat Caleb was his nickname,
  Terror of the seven seas.

Caleb's beard was black and curly,
  He had several nasty scars;
He was short but very burly –
  For a hobby he bent bars.

Caleb had a sense of humour,
  Liked to make men walk the plank;
Loved to see the sharks arriving,
  And the bubbles when ships sank.

Both had heard much of the other,
  Though the pair had never met.
Then one summer, off Jamaica,
  Just before the sun did set. . .

Annie's ship bore down on Caleb's,
  Shots rang out and cannons roared;
But when Annie through a spyglass
  Spotted Caleb – her heart soared!

Caleb meanwhile was observing
   His opponent with desire.
Then to his fierce crew's amazement,
   Caleb told them to cease fire.

Annie grabbed a handy halyard,
   Bellowed out a war-like cry,
Swung across and flattened Caleb.
   (Annie never had been shy.)

Caleb jumped up, laughed and welcomed
   Annie to his privateer,
Asked her if she'd stay for dinner –
   Salt pork, biscuits, lots of beer.

Soon the pirates were like lovebirds.
   In a week they'd set a date.
What a wedding! What a couple!
   Each had found the perfect mate.

Love was blooming, and now Nature
   Enters in our pirate tale. . .
Late one night *The Jolly Herbert*
   Echoed to a baby's wail.

Now the pirates had a daughter;
   Polly was the name they chose.
She was perfect, and her parents
   Loved her little turned-up nose.

For a while the crew was happy;
   Newborns' needs are very slight.
Things, though, worsened rather
                     quickly. . .
   Polly woke up *every* night.

Polly screamed and gave them headaches,
   From her nappies wafted smells
That were worse than unwashed pirates;
   Made them sicker than sea swells.

Annie organized a rota,
   Each crew member took his turn
Washing nappies, feeding Polly,
   Walking her from bow to stern.

Soon the crew was feeling angry,
   Said they didn't want to be
Babyminders – they were pirates. . .
   So they staged a mutiny.

Annie fought, and Caleb struggled,
   But defeat was sure and swift;
With their baby in a dinghy
   They were thrown . . . then cast adrift!

All alone out on the briny
   Bobbed the dinghy, small and frail;
But our heroes didn't panic –
   They had soon rigged up a sail.

Annie did the navigation,
   Caleb steered, and with a toe
Rocked young Polly in her cradle.
   Then he called out, 'Look, land ho!'

They had made it to the mainland,
    But they didn't plan to stay;
Once they had a ship to sail on
    They would make those traitors pay.

Life, alas, is seldom simple;
    Sometimes troubles never end.
In the harbour our brave couple
    Found themselves without a friend.

Not one single pirate captain
    Offered them a berth aboard;
They caused mirth at every gunwale,
    All the buccaneers guffawed,

Said that parents can't be pirates,
    Ships and babies were opposed;
Caleb pleaded, Annie cursed them,
    But their hearts and minds were closed.

Our brave couple thus were thwarted;
    That was that, conclusively.
They must give up being pirates,
    Which they did – reluctantly.

So they settled down to normal
   Life upon the lubber's shore,
Bought a house in Seaview Crescent.
   It was number 44.

When the pair ran out of treasure
   Annie found a job that paid,
Working in a busy office
   Dealing with the shipping trade.

Caleb cooked and did the shopping,
    Cared for Polly, kept her clean;
He became the most domestic
    Pirate that there's ever been.

Time went by, and our ex-pirates
    Often felt that life was dull.
Sometimes, from their little cottage,
    They would watch a wheeling gull. . .

Office days were long and weary,
  Paper piled up, things to do.
No-one ever sang a shanty,
  Not like their old pirate crew.

Going shopping was so boring.
  How they missed their life at sea!
Whistling wind and salt waves crashing –
  Pirates' lives were wild and free.

Polly thrived though, that's what mattered,
  Grew to be their special girl;
Tough and strong, just like her mother,
  Hair like Caleb's, with a curl.

Not for Polly pirate habits.
  She was going off to school,
Where the teacher, Mrs Primly,
  Taught them all The Golden Rule:

Always search out hidden talent;
  Set yourself the sternest test.
Find the thing you can excel at;
  Then make sure you do it best.

Polly was a quiet pupil,
    Did her work and just got by.
Mrs Primly thought her. . . average,
    And, what's more, a trifle shy.

Then one day there was an outing
    To a park that had a lake;
Mrs Primly didn't know it,
    But she'd made a *big* mistake.

First they studied trees and flowers,
    After that they ate their lunch.
Then the plan was for some boating,
    As they were a placid bunch.

But when Polly saw her rowboat
    Something happened to the child;
She became a different person,
    Nostrils flaring, eyes gone wild.

Polly roared and showed her tonsils,
    Talked of anchors, raising sail;
Then she spat and cursed her teacher.
    Mrs Primly turned quite pale.

Polly held up all her classmates
    As they stood there on the bank,
Emptied Mrs Primly's handbag,
    Then she made her walk the plank.

It took several large policemen
    To arrest the wildcat girl;
They arrived with sirens blaring,
    But she led them such a whirl.

When they caught her she was vicious,
   Punched and pounded, bashed and bit;
Knocked one sergeant quite unconscious.
   Eyes were blackened, lips were split.

Later, Caleb got a summons.
   He and Annie went to school,
Where they talked to Mrs Primly,
   Who was stern (and *very* cool).

She revealed their daughter's actions,
   Told them of the sorry tale;
Said the child was like a pirate!
   Mentioned she'd been thrown in jail.

Cut-throat Caleb sat there silent.
   Keel-haul Annie did the same.
Both were distant, thinking deeply. . .
   Neither felt a shred of shame.

Now they saw that their sweet Polly
   Was like them down to the core;
Pirate parents, pirate daughter –
   Pirates all, for ever more!

Suddenly a stone was lifted
   From their souls, and they were free;
It was simple – they should stick to
   Doing what comes naturally!

So they tied up Mrs Primly,
   Bust their daughter out of jail,
Shot the town up, burnt the school down,
   Stole a ship and then set sail.

They tracked down *The Jolly Herbert*,
   Boarded their old pirate ship;
Got the crew obeying orders. . .
   Annie used her trusty whip!

All the rest is pirate history;
   Books are full of what they did.
They defeated every legend –
   Blackbeard, Bonny, Cap'n Kidd,

And amassed a heap of treasure,
    But they didn't really care.
It was great just being pirates –
    Freedom, fun and salty air,

Battles, broadsides, desert islands,
    Living on the ocean waves;
Not for them a life of shopping,
    School, or being office slaves.

Polly, though, absorbed one lesson
    Very well at her old school.
She became the greatest pirate
    Thanks to Primly's Golden Rule.

She would never be a scholar.
    She would never learn to spell.
But she knew that as a pirate
    She would always . . . well, *excel*.

Polly grew, became an adult,
    Worked hard at her pirate skills;
Just the news that she had landed
    Sent men screaming to the hills. . .

. . . All but one, a fierce young rascal;
   Tall and strong, his name was Bart.
Polly saw him in her spyglass,
   And, like Annie, lost her heart.

Soon, perhaps, a second baby
   Will be born and loudly wail. . .
But it's time to end *this* story –
   That would be another tale!

Tony Bradman